TEACHING THE BIBLE

Practical help for Bible teachers and preachers around the world

Written by
David Sprouse

PPP: Teaching the Bible
© David Sprouse / The Good Book Company, 2015.

email: ppp@thegoodbook.co.uk

Published by
The Good Book Company

Websites:
UK: www.thegoodbook.co.uk
North America: www.thegoodbook.com
Australia: www.thegoodbook.com.au
New Zealand: www.thegoodbook.co.nz

ISBN: 9781784980078

Printed in India

The PPP project is working in partnership with a growing number of organisations worldwide, including: Langham Partnership • Grace Baptist Mission • Pastor Training International (PTI) • Sovereign World Trust • Africa Inland Mission (AIM) • Worldshare • Entrust Foundation • India Bible Literature • African Pastors' Book Fund • Preacher's Help • African Christian Textbooks (ACTS) Nigeria • Orphans for Christ, Uganda • Project Timothy.

Also in the PPP series:

PPP God's Big Story • PPP Mark • PPP Philippians • PPP Job • PPP 2 Timothy • PPP Deuteronomy • PPP Acts

Contents

WELCOME TO *PPP:* TEACHING THE BIBLE

In this book we will learn how to study and preach the Bible, but there is something more important to God and to your hearers—**how you live your life**. It is important to take care of our **lives** as well as our **teaching**.

1 Timothy 4:12-16 says:

> [12]Don't let anyone look down on you because you are young, but set an example for the believers in speech, in conduct, in love, in faith and in purity. [13]Until I come, devote yourself to the public reading of Scripture, to preaching and to teaching. [14]Do not neglect your gift, which was given you through prophecy when the body of elders laid their hands on you. [15]Be diligent in these matters; give yourself wholly to them, so that everyone may see your progress. [16]Watch your life and doctrine closely. Persevere in them, because if you do, you will save both yourself and your hearers.

Paul wrote to Timothy, who was leading the church at Ephesus. These verses give important instructions to all pastors and preachers. In verses 13-15 Paul talks about the job of a pastor: he is to read the Bible to the church, and to preach and teach it. In verse 12 and verse 16 Paul talks about the Bible teacher's life.

- *In what ways is a Bible teacher to set a good example? (v12)*

- *What must the Bible teacher watch (be very careful about)? (v16)*

Paul says Timothy is to set a good example. He is not only to **say** what the Bible says, but also to **show** what the Bible says by the way he lives.

Paul says Timothy must "watch his life and doctrine". To "watch your life" means to be very careful to walk closely with God and follow what the Bible says. To "watch your doctrine" means to be very careful to believe and teach what the Bible says.

Think about your life:

- *What kind of example are you in your words, how you behave, your love, your faith, your purity?*
- *What do others see in your life?*
- *What do others hear in your teaching? Do you stick closely to the Bible?*

It is wonderful to be a pastor or preacher, to speak God's word! But there are many dangers. Sadly, many pastors and preachers do not take care of their lives. They do not take care to keep close to God.

Time with God

The most important relationship in your life is your relationship with God. If you do not take care of it you will be in danger. Many preachers only read the Bible to prepare a sermon. They are very busy but they do not pray. Make sure to spend time every day reading the Bible and praying on your own.

Read the Bible so **you** can listen to God. This is not study time. This is to deepen your relationship with your heavenly Father. Do not think of your sermon or what other people need to hear. Listen to God speak to **you** as you read.

Read how great God is and how sinful you are. Read what Jesus has done for you when he died on the cross, taking the punishment for your sin so you can be forgiven. Read how God calls you to love him and love people. Read that Jesus is coming again and you will meet him.

These truths will keep you from pride as you remember that you are not great, but a sinner saved by grace. You are not a great preacher who is very important, but a helpless sinner who needs God's grace and power. These truths will help you be loving and pure and not greedy.

A pastor, leader or preacher must first learn to listen to God. They must teach themselves before they teach others.

1. WHAT IS THE BIBLE?

In this chapter we will learn:

- The Bible is God's precious word. It is the most wonderful book in the world!

- The Bible is for everyone, everywhere.

● *What is the most precious thing you have in your house?*

Psalm 19:7-11 says:

> *⁷The law of the LORD is perfect, refreshing the soul. The statutes of the LORD are trustworthy, making wise the simple. ⁸The precepts of the LORD are right, giving joy to the heart. The commands of the LORD are radiant, giving light to the eyes. ⁹The fear of the LORD is pure, enduring for ever. The decrees of the LORD are firm, and all of them are righteous. ¹⁰They are more precious than gold, than much pure gold; they are sweeter than honey, than honey from the honeycomb. ¹¹By them your servant is warned; in keeping them there is great reward.*

The psalm uses different words for God's word (law, statutes, precepts, commands, decrees).

These words all mean God's word, the Bible.

*Read **Psalm 19:7-11** again*

- ● *What does the psalm say about God's word?*

- ● *Why does the psalm say that God's word is like gold and honey (v10)?*

The Bible is more precious than lots of gold or money or treasure (v10). To have a Bible is to have the most precious thing in the world! When you read it, you find real treasure. God's word refreshes or gives life to the soul (v7). It gives joy to the heart, and it gives light so we can see where to go (v8).

When you are very hungry, you feel tired. It is hard to be hungry and happy. But when at last you have some food, it changes how you feel and gives energy to your body. The Bible is like that. It is like sweet honey (v10), full of goodness for our souls, giving us strength to live for God.

The Bible is God's word

When we read the Bible, we are listening to God talk to us.

Think about that. How does that make you feel?

God is very great. He is the Creator of everything—seen and unseen. There is no one more important to listen to. When we read our Bibles, we listen to GOD speak to us!

In Psalm 19:1-6 we read that the stars, moon, sun and planets tell us how great God is.

We can see from God's creation that God is very powerful, wise and great. But it is only in the Bible we see how holy and loving he is. It is only in the Bible we find how we can know him.

The Bible is for everyone

Everywhere in the world we feel the sun and see the stars. In the same way the Bible is God's book for everyone everywhere. The Bible is not a white man's book or a book for clever people. The Bible is for everyone. In the Bible we meet people from all over the world. The Bible was first written in the Hebrew and Greek languages, and read by people in the Middle-East, in Asia and Africa and Europe. It was only translated into English about 500 years ago!

Read these verses and ask God to help YOU to understand how precious and important the Bible is:

> *I have treasured the words of his (God's) mouth more than my daily bread. (Job 23:12)*

> *Open my eyes that I may see wonderful things in your law. (Psalm 119:18)*

> *Your word is a lamp for my feet, a light on my path. (Psalm 119:105)*

> *For the word of God is alive and active … it judges the thoughts and attitudes of the heart. (Hebrews 4:12)*

Think of a man who is very hungry. You give him food. He takes it but does not eat it. He puts it in a box and does not touch it. Seven days later you hear that the man died of hunger. You will think: "Why didn't he eat the food I gave him?"

Many people treat the Bible like this. They have a Bible but they do not read it. They hold the Bible but they do not open it! God's word is food for YOU! But you will only be fed and helped if you read it. It is best to read it every day.

Imagine a woman who says that she loves her husband. But she does not listen to him. Every time he speaks, she walks away. When he tries to make her listen, she starts singing and does not hear what he says. How will the man feel?

How does God feel when we do not spend time listening to him? If you love Jesus, you must listen to Jesus! He has given you his word so that you can hear him every day!

THINK
- *Is the Bible the most precious thing you have?*
- *Will you spend 15 minutes each day reading the Bible and listening to God?*
- *Will you read the Bible and find how to better love and follow Jesus?*

One God, One World, One Book

How the Bible came to us

- God, by his Holy Spirit, helped about 40 different people to write the Bible over 1500 years.

- The Old Testament was completed 400 years before Jesus was born and was written in Hebrew.

- The New Testament was completed 50 years after Jesus died and rose. It was written in Greek.

- We do not have the original books that, for example, Moses, Isaiah, Mark or Paul wrote, but we do have many copies and some of them are very old.

- The copies were made very carefully. By comparing them we can see how very carefully the copies were made.

- The Hebrew and Greek have been translated into many different languages. The whole Bible is translated into over 500 different languages and the New Testament into 1300 languages. More translations are still needed!

- The Bible is **God's word**—God is the author. Every word is true. God has cared for the Bible so we can read it. We can trust it is the true words of the living God. Be sure to listen to what God wants us to hear.

2. TEACH THE BIBLE

In this chapter we will learn:

- Teaching the Bible is the most important thing that happens in church.
- God changes lives when the Bible is taught well.
- Teaching the Bible is hard work—it takes time to prepare a good message.

2 Timothy 3:16-17 says:

[16]All Scripture is God-breathed and is useful for teaching, rebuking, correcting and training in righteousness, [17]so that the servant of God may be thoroughly equipped for every good work.

- *What do these verses say about Scripture (the Bible)?*
- *What is the Bible useful for?*

Teaching the Bible is very important

Imagine the president of your country sends you a message. Imagine you get a letter from a rich relative in America. You will be very excited. You will tell everyone!

The Bible is a letter from GOD to you. The Bible (Scripture) IS God's message. It is "God-breathed". Think about your words. They come out of your mouth. Your breath is in them. The Bible comes from God. Every word has God's breath in it.

This means the Bible is true, powerful and useful.

1. The Bible is true

Does God ever make a mistake? Does God ever change his mind? No! God is holy and right. He does not change. God does not need to change—he is perfect! Everything God says is always true. We are not perfect. We get many things wrong. The only way to find what is right is to listen to God. The way to listen to God is to read or listen to the Bible.

Many churches do not listen carefully to the Bible. Many pastors do not teach what the Bible says. They say what they think is right. Many churches around the world do not know what is right because they do not listen carefully to the Bible. Many Christians believe wrong things and do wrong things because they do not listen carefully to the Bible. What about you?

2. The Bible is powerful

How did God create the world? In Genesis 1:3, God said: "Let there be light", and there was light. God's words are very powerful. Through God's word all the world was made! (Genesis 1) Through God's words people are saved and changed. The Bible changes people to become more like Jesus.

Do you want people to be saved? Do you want the believers in your church to be more like Jesus? Do you want the young Christians in your church to be pure? So what must you do? You must teach the Bible with care and kindness. God's word is the most important thing for your people to hear.

3. The Bible is useful

Read 2 Timothy 3:16 again.

If you want to catch a fish, then a net or fishing line is useful. If you want to cook dinner, then some vegetables and a pot is useful. The Bible is useful. It is helpful. In 2 Timothy 3:16 Paul tells Timothy four ways the Bible is useful so people are equipped or ready to serve God (v17).

- It is useful for teaching—the Bible tells us what is right.

- It is useful for rebuking—the Bible tells us what is wrong.

- It is useful for correcting—the Bible tells us how to leave the wrong way.

- It is useful for training in righteousness—the Bible tell us how to live a right life.

The Bible is God's word. It is true. It is powerful. It is useful. To read and teach the Bible is very important and very exciting. When we teach the Bible with prayer and care, people will be saved, believers will be changed and God will be praised!

Teaching the Bible is hard work

2 Timothy 2:15 says:

> *Do your best to present yourself to God as one approved, a worker who does not need to be ashamed and who correctly handles (explains) the word of truth.*

- *Paul writes to Timothy, who is a church leader in Ephesus. What does Paul tell him to do?*
- *Paul uses the picture of a worker. What does this tell us about teaching the Bible?*

Imagine an important man gives you a message. He says: "Tell your village that on Wednesday there is free bread at the market at 6am". But you are in a different village. You are tired. You do not go and tell the message. Or maybe, you tell the message but tell everyone to come on Thursday. It is the wrong message! How will the people feel? How will the important man feel?

A sermon is the message you will teach. Are you giving the wrong message in your sermons because you do not work hard to understand and teach the Bible? God's message is very important and must be passed on clearly. God's message is better than free bread!

Paul says Bible teachers are to be faithful workers. A worker is someone who works hard. Teaching the Bible is hard work. It makes you tired. It takes many hours to prepare a good message. But many teachers and preachers spend only a few minutes preparing a message. This is not good. They are not good workers. Imagine a man builds a wall. He is lazy. He does a bad job and the wall falls down. He is not a reliable worker. No one will want him to work for them!

You must work hard to "correctly handle the word of truth". What happens if you carry a bucket of water upside down? You are carrying the bucket but you do not correctly handle it. Many preachers use the Bible in a bad way. They do not correctly explain it. They do not listen to what the Bible says. They say what they want to say, or what people want to hear. This is very bad. We must correctly explain the Bible—God's precious word. This takes hard work and many hours of study. We must be humble and first learn from God ourselves. Many preachers are proud. They think they know what is right. To be good preachers and teachers who please God we must be humble and careful to study well.

Learning from this book will be hard work. But it is very important. It is also very exciting! Great things happen when God's word is taught well!

THINK

- *How much time do you spend reading the Bible?*

- *Do you use the Bible to show people the message about Jesus?*

- *How long did you take to prepare your last sermon or talk?*

- *Do you need to confess to God that you have not been a faithful, hard-working preacher?*

Teach the Bible only!

There is only **ONE** true God
and only **ONE** book from God—the Bible.

The Bible is **COMPLETE**. It says **ALL** you need to know about God. We must **never add** other teaching to the Bible.

God **MADE** us. He **loves** and knows what is best for us. We must follow his ways and not our ways or the way that other people follow.

God is the **KING**. The Bible tells us his rules. We must obey it MORE than the traditions of our cultures or churches.

The Bible speaks **CLEARLY**. Everyone can read and understand it. Do not follow a teaching if the Bible does not clearly teach it.

3. TEACH ALL THE BIBLE

In this chapter we will see that:

- The Bible is ONE story—God's story.

- Every book in the Bible is about Jesus.

- It is good to teach from ALL the books in the Bible but we must see where each book fits in the Bible's big story.

> **Luke 24:44-49** says:
>
> [44]*He (Jesus) said to them, "This is what I told you while I was still with you: everything must be fulfilled that is written about me in the Law of Moses, the Prophets and the Psalms."* [45]*Then he opened their minds so they could understand the Scriptures.* [46]*He told them, "This is what is written: the Messiah will suffer and rise from the dead on the third day,* [47]*and repentance for the forgiveness of sins will be preached in his name to all nations, beginning at Jerusalem.* [48]*You are witnesses of these things.* [49]*I am going to send you what my Father has promised; but stay in the city until you have been clothed with power from on high."*
>
> ● *What does Jesus say is written in the Scriptures?*
>
> ● *What message does Jesus say will be preached?*

Jesus is speaking to his disciples after he has risen from the dead. In Luke 24:44 Jesus says to them: *"This is what I told you while I was still with you: everything must be fulfilled that is written about me in the Law of Moses, the Prophets and the Psalms."*

One big promise

Jesus speaks of the Law of Moses, the Prophets and the Psalms. This means the Old Testament. Jesus tells his disciples the Old Testament is about HIM. The words "must be fulfilled" mean "must take place." All the promises and pictures about Jesus in the Old Testament had to take place.

The whole Bible is all about Jesus.

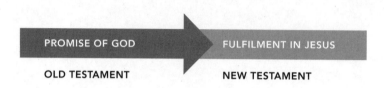

PROMISE OF GOD → FULFILMENT IN JESUS

OLD TESTAMENT — NEW TESTAMENT

The Old Testament shows God's great plan to save the world through Jesus. It shows what Jesus will do and what he will be like.

The New Testament shows how Jesus came and fulfilled God's great plan by his perfect life, his death on the cross, his resurrection and return to heaven.

In the Old Testament, God shows this promise in:

- *words* (for example: Genesis 3:15, 12:1-7, Micah 5:2, Isaiah 53)
- *people* (for example: the people of Israel, David)
- *events* (for example: Passover, crossing the Red Sea)
- *places* (for example: the Promised Land, the temple)
- *practices* (for example: sacrifices, festivals)

In the New Testament, God fulfils his promise through Jesus. You can see this in:

- *words* (Jesus does exactly what God promises. For example: Matthew says: "So was fulfilled what was said..." Matthew 2:17, 2:23, 13:14, 13:35, 26:54, 26:56, 27:9)
- *people* (Jesus is our Prophet, Priest and King)
- *events* (Jesus died and rose again to rescue us and bring us to God)
- *places* (to come close to God we do not go to a temple, we go to Jesus)
- *practices* (Jesus' death fulfils all the pictures of the sacrifices)

Remember, the Old Testament shows what God is like, what we are like and what God promised Jesus will do to save us and make us his people.

"Passage" means the verses we will study or preach from. For any passage we read, it is always good to ask:

- *how does this passage show us what God is like?*

- *how does this passage show us our sin?*

- *how does this passage show us what Jesus would need to do to bring us to God?*

- *how does this passage show us what it means to be the people of God?*

One big story

To understand any book we must know where it fits in the Bible's big story.

The diagrams on pages 18-19 will help you with this.

One book at a time

A good way to teach the Bible is to work through a whole book, one passage after another. For example, the book of Mark. You start with Mark 1:1-8; then the next time teach Mark 1:9-15; then Mark 1:16-20, then Mark 1:21-28, then Mark 1:29-45 and so on.

This is a good way because:

- you can see more clearly how the book fits in the Bible's big story.

- you and your hearers can see how the message of the book fits together.

- you are preaching God's message as he has given it to us, rather than you choosing what you want to say.

- you speak about passages and topics you would never choose to preach from.

This will mean that you and your church learn more from God's word.

This is the model that we use in the *Pray Prepare Preach* series. Some books of the Bible are very long, so you may do part of a book and then teach something different, and then come back to the first book again.

It is good to have a balance of teaching from different parts of the Bible, from the Old Testament and from the New Testament. Then your hearers learn all that the Bible says.

One big story

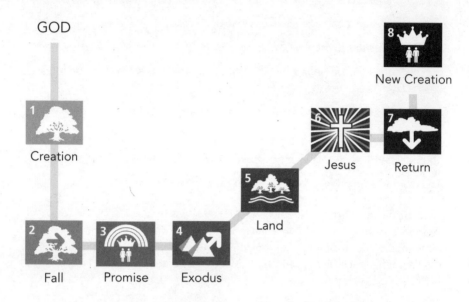

This shows the eight main events in the Bible story.

This shows how man goes away from God and how God brings his people back. See that **8. New Creation** is higher than **1. Creation**. This is to show that God brings us even closer to him than Adam and Eve were in the garden. The new creation (a new heaven and a new earth) is much better than the first creation was!

OLD TESTAMENT
God creates everything good. (Genesis 1 – 2)

God creates the first people. He is friends with them in a beautiful garden.

Man sins and now cannot be friends with God. (Genesis 3 – 11)

Adam and Eve go against what God told them. The Bible calls this sin. Sin brings death into the world. Now man cannot be friends with God.

Promise

God's special promise to Abraham. (Genesis 12 – 50)

God promises Abraham that he will make people friends with God again. God promises them a homeland, where he will be with them and bless them.

Exodus

God rescues his people from Egypt. (Exodus to Deuteronomy)

The people of Israel are Abraham's family line. God says they are his special people. They become slaves in Egypt. God rescues his people from Egypt. They travel to the Promised Land.

Land

God blesses his people in the Promised Land. (Joshua to Malachi)

God brings his people into the Promised Land. They defeat the Canaanites. God blesses them. But they worship false gods. God gives them trouble from the nations round them. In the end, enemies take God's people away to foreign lands. They return, but they still sin. They need a Saviour to save them from their sin.

NEW TESTAMENT

Jesus

God sends Jesus to save people everywhere. (Matthew to Acts)

Jesus comes to die on a cross and rise from the dead. This is the only answer for our sin. This is the only way God and man can be friends again.

Return

Jesus will return to end the world and judge everyone. (Romans to Revelation 19)

People who follow Jesus are friends with God. But it is not easy to follow Jesus. Satan is against us. We look forward to when Jesus will come back. Jesus will make everything right.

New Creation

God's people will be perfect friends with God for ever. (Revelation 20 – 22)

God will punish everyone who has not trusted Jesus. God will send them away from him for ever, to hell. God's people will live with him in the new heavens and new earth. They will love and serve Jesus for ever. God's promise will come true completely.

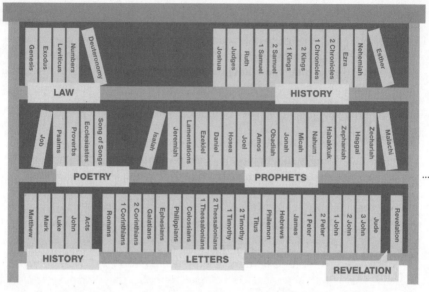

All the Bible is God's word. All the Bible teaches us about Jesus. But there are different kinds of books:

- **History** — A history book is a book of true stories. It is a historical narrative. This means true stories about people who lived a long time ago.

- **Law of Moses** — It is very important to remember we are NOT the old covenant people of God. There are many laws in the Law of Moses that do not apply to us today. We follow only laws which also come in the New Testament.

- **Poetry** — A poem is different from a story. Poems and songs show how we feel. Songs and poems use language in a different way to stories. They use words as pictures.

- **Prophets** — The prophets were men who God gave a message to for God's people. The prophets reminded the people of what God HAD said in the Old Testament law. The prophets told the people what God WILL do in the future.

- **Letters** — There are 21 letters in the New Testament. Thirteen of the letters were written by Paul. The letters help us to understand and live out the message of Jesus.

- **Revelation** — Revelation means something hidden is now seen. Revelation shows what is happening in the world and in heaven now, and what will happen when Jesus comes again.

Where to start

All the Bible is God's word but some books are easier to teach than others. Some parts are more helpful to God's people.

Here are some books and sections that are very important for our understanding of God and the message about Jesus:

- Genesis 1-12 — Creation, fall, flood, promise to Abraham

- Exodus 1-20 — rescue from slavery

- Psalms 1-2 — these psalms introduce all the other psalms

- Isaiah 53 — a wonderful promise about the cross

- Mark — the shortest Gospel

- Acts 1-2 — the coming of the Holy Spirit

- Ephesians — a letter about the church: God's people saved by grace, called to live for him

- 1 John — we show we are God's people by believing in Jesus and loving one another

ACTION

- *How much of the Bible have you read?*

- *Will you plan to read the whole Bible? Ask another pastor or teacher to also read like this so you can help each other.*

4. PRAY

This book is in a series called "**Pray** Prepare Preach" (PPP).

In this chapter we learn:

- We **must** PRAY as we study God's word.

- We need the help of the Holy Spirit to understand and teach God's word.

- We must PRAY for the Holy Spirit to use God's words to change people as they hear God's word.

- PRAYING is **so** important. It is **so** easy for PRAYING to get missed out.

---

1 Thessalonians 1:4-5 says:

⁴For we know, brothers and sisters loved by God, that he has chosen you, ⁵because our gospel came to you not simply with words but also with power, with the Holy Spirit and deep conviction. You know how we lived among you for your sake.

(Note: "conviction" means they knew it was true.)

- *How did the gospel (good news) come to them?*

- *What did the Holy Spirit do when Paul brought the good news to them?*

Paul preached the good news to the people at Thessalonica. A few months later he wrote a letter to them. He tells them he remembers speaking the good news to them and he gives thanks to God for them (v2). He thanks God because when he preached the good news to them, they welcomed the message. In verse 9 Paul says they turned "from idols to serve the living and true God". Why did they do this? Verse 5 gives us the answer. The Holy Spirit helped them to be sure the message was true ("conviction").

These verses teach us that two things are needed for people to become believers:

1. The message of Jesus

2. The Holy Spirit

Paul says the gospel (the message of Jesus) "came to you not simply with words but also with power." For people to believe, we must explain the message. Words to explain the good news are needed. But this is not enough. For people to believe and be saved, the Holy Spirit is needed. He uses the words to change people's hearts.

We cannot change people's hearts. Only God can do that.

We cannot make people believe. Only God can do that.

The best sermon will not help people if the Holy Spirit does not work. We need the Holy Spirit to help us to:

- prepare to teach the Bible.

- preach and teach the Bible.

We need the Holy Spirit to help us and our hearers to:

- understand the Bible.

- believe the Bible.

- live out the message of the Bible.

We need the Holy Spirit's help and so we **must** PRAY!

Pray and prepare

We must PRAY *before* we PREPARE.

Pray you will hear God speak to *you*. Pray the Holy Spirit will help you to understand the Bible. Remember, the Holy Spirit helped those who wrote down the Bible (2 Peter 1:21) and he can help you to understand the Bible.

Pray the Holy Spirit will help you to hear the message yourself before you speak the message to others.

There will be times as you study the Bible when you do not understand the passage. Every preacher around the world finds this! Some passages are very hard to understand. When you do not understand, ask God to help you. Keep reading the passage. Read it aloud. Pray about each sentence. If you ask God to help you, he will.

Pray and preach

We must PRAY *before* we speak.

Preaching and teaching God's word is a very important job. Remember, God is listening. We want to say what God says. We want people to hear God speak and not only us!

Pray you will speak God's truth clearly.

Pray before you go to the meeting. Ask some people to pray with you before the meeting starts.

Pray with your hearers before you give the message.

Pray and pray

We must PRAY *after* we teach God's word.

Thank God for his help and pray your hearers will respond to God's word.

THINK

- *Why **must** you pray for God's help as you prepare?*
- *Why **must** you pray for God's help as you preach?*
- *What will you pray to God about now?*

5. HOW TO PREPARE A SERMON OR TALK

This book is in a series called "Pray **Prepare** Preach".

In the next three chapters:

- We learn how to PREPARE a sermon or talk.

- There are three parts:

    □ Chapter 6—how to STUDY a section or passage of the Bible so we understand what the message from God is.

    □ Chapter 7—how to PLAN a talk on a passage of the Bible so our hearers will hear God's message.

    □ Chapter 8—how to prepare notes to TEACH a passage of the Bible clearly.

2 Timothy 2:15 says:

Do your best to present yourself to God as one approved, a worker who does not need to be ashamed and who correctly handles the word of truth.

- *Why does Paul tell Timothy to be a "worker"?*

- *What does it mean to "do your best"?*

A worker will work all day doing his job. He works hard. He gets tired and hungry. That's the same for God's workers! It is hard work to prepare a Bible talk or sermon. It takes many hours. "Do your best" means to work hard and do the very best you can. It means to study and study and study. This book helps you but it does not do all the work for you!

You need to read the passage slowly. You need to study the verses carefully. You need to prepare what you will say to your hearers so they will be helped. Take as much time as you can to prepare a talk or sermon. Preparing a good talk or sermon may take a whole day!

PRAY

Pray for God's help

STUDY

1. Study to **UNDERSTAND** the Bible section

2. READ the Bible section several times

3. Think about the **BACKGROUND**

4. Try to find the **MAIN POINT OF THE PASSAGE** that God is teaching us in the Bible section

PLAN

1. Plan your Bible talk

2. Work out **THE MAIN POINT OF THE SERMON**

3. Plan your **SUB-POINTS** and how you will **ILLUSTRATE** and **APPLY** the **MAIN POINT**

TEACH

1. Prepare your talk to give it in your own language. Make notes to help you

2. **Write notes on how you will START, EXPLAIN** and **END** your talk

REVIEW

1. Is the **MAIN POINT** clear?

2. Do you show what the Bible teaches in **THAT** passage?

3. Have you explained the verses clearly?

4. Have you thought of word pictures to help people understand and remember?

5. Do you connect with the people?

6. What are you asking God to change in the lives of your hearers?

PRAY

1. Pray that God will speak through your words

2. Pray that God's truth will change people

6. STUDY
HOW TO UNDERSTAND THE PASSAGE

In this chapter:

- We begin to learn how to **prepare** a sermon or talk.

- We will look at how to STUDY a section or passage of the Bible so we understand what the message from God is.

- We will learn that we must find **one MAIN POINT** from the passage.

Follow these steps to study a passage:

BACKGROUND → READ → UNDERSTAND → Find the MAIN POINT of the passage

The Bible is God's word. When we teach the Bible, we must make sure people hear what God says. This means we must be very careful to find the **MAIN POINT** of a passage—because that is what God wants us to say! When you know the **MAIN POINT**, you will know what God wants you to say. Then you can think how best to apply it to your hearers.

So how do you find the **MAIN POINT**? Follow the steps on the next page:

BACKGROUND

Think about the **BACKGROUND** to the passage.

What do we mean by **BACKGROUND**? Here is an illustration: look at the first picture of a plane. What can you say about where the plane is?

Now look at this second picture. It is the same picture but now you can see the **BACKGROUND**. What can you say about where the plane is?

You can see that the plane has landed. It is near a village. The sky is dark and it is a dangerous time to fly so it must be an important journey.

The **BACKGROUND** makes a big difference to understanding. So, when we study God's word we need to see the **BACKGROUND** to the passage.

This has three parts:

1. Where in the **story** of the Bible the passage comes

2. Where in the **book** of the Bible the passage comes

3. What happens in the **chapters** or **verses** before and after the passage

When we know these things, we understand the Bible passage better.

A sermon is usually from a few verses or one chapter. These verses fit into the whole chapter, and into the whole book and into the whole Bible! Think how a passage builds on what was said before.

To understand the **BACKGROUND** you need to think about:

The whole Bible

- Where in the story of the Bible does this book come?

- Is it in the Old Testament (before Jesus came) or in the New Testament (when or after Jesus came)?

- When in history is this book set? (The Bible story is the true history of the world.)
  - ☐ References and footnotes may also help you see how this passage fits into the whole Bible.

Example—Genesis 12:1-9

☐ *Genesis is the first book of the Old Testament.*

☐ *Genesis tells the story of the world from the beginning.*

☐ *Genesis 12 is a long time before Jesus came.*

The whole book

- Who wrote the book?

- Who was the book written for?
  - ☐ In many New Testament books you find help in the first verses of the book.
  - ☐ You may find help in the introduction to the book in your Bible.

Example—Genesis 12:1-9

☐ *Genesis is the first of the five books of Moses.*

☐ *Moses wrote these books for the Old Testament people of God.*

The passage before the one you will speak from

- Where is it in the book?

- What is the main point of the passage before this one?

Example—Genesis 12:1-9

☐ *Genesis chapters 3 – 11 are about sin and judgment. God has made the world. Sin has spoiled the world. God has judged the world with a flood. People have not turned to God. The people built the Tower of Babel to make a name for themselves. They did not honour God's name. They did not follow what God said. God punishes them by making them all speak different languages, and so they spread out as God told them.*

☐ *In Genesis 11:27-32 we are told about Abram (who will later be called Abraham) and his family. We learn that Abraham is married to Sarah and they have no children. We learn they leave their home to go to Canaan.*

☐ *The background is very important. Genesis chapters 3 – 11 show people are sinners. They do not deserve good things from God. People reject God. They deserve to be sent away from God. In Genesis 12 God shows great love and grace. God promises to bless (to do good to) the world. Abraham does not deserve to be blessed. God begins to work out his amazing plan for a sinful world.*

READ
Genesis 12:1-9

¹The LORD had said to Abram, "Go from your country, your people and your father's household and go to the land I will show you. ²"I will make you into a great nation, and I will bless you; I will make your name great, and you will be a blessing. ³I will bless those who bless you, and whoever curses you I will curse; and all peoples on earth will be blessed through you." ⁴So Abram left, as the LORD had told him; and Lot went with him. Abram was seventy-five years old when he set out from Harran. ⁵He took his wife Sarai, his nephew Lot, all the possessions they had accumulated and the people they had acquired in Harran, and they set out for the land of Canaan, and they arrived there. ⁶Abram travelled through the land as far as the site of the great tree of Moreh at Shechem. At that time the Canaanites were in the land. ⁷The LORD appeared to Abram and said, "To your offspring I will give this land." So he built an altar there to the LORD, who had appeared to him. ⁸From there he went on towards the hills east of Bethel and pitched his tent, with Bethel on the west and Ai on the east. There he built an altar to the LORD and called on the name of the LORD. ⁹Then Abram set out and continued towards the Negev.

READ the Bible passage **three times**. READ it slowly and carefully. It is best to READ out loud. READ it in a different translation if you have one. The third time READ it with your eyes and ears, your nose and hands! Imagine you were there. What will you see, hear, smell and feel?

What words are difficult? Try and work out what they mean. Is there someone you can ask to help you? Can you look in a dictionary? The PPP books have notes to help with this.

Example—Genesis 12:1-9

☐ *Verse 5: "the possessions they had **accumulated** and the people they had* ***acquired****"—this means they took everything they had! "Accumulated" means "collected", and "acquired" means "bought".*

☐ *Verse 7: "offspring" means "child/children" or "descendant(s)".*

UNDERSTAND

Work on UNDERSTANDING the passage. To teach a passage well you need to understand clearly what it says.

Look carefully at this picture of the plane. What can you learn about what **is** happening?

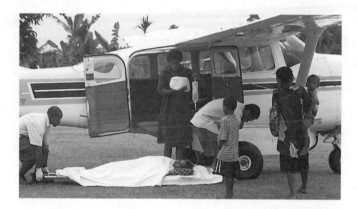

In the same way you must spend time carefully seeing what the passage **does** say.

Go through verse by verse. Read each verse and then say what happens in your own words. This helps you to know what the passage is about.

Now look at the picture again. What does the picture **not** tell you? For example, you do not know what the sick person is suffering with.

In the same way **do not** guess about what the passage does **not** say.

Here are some questions to ask:

Who?
Who is in this passage?

- What do you learn about each of the people?

- What do you learn about where they are?

- What does this passage say about God (Father, Jesus and Holy Spirit)?

What?
What is it about?

- Are any words or ideas repeated?

- Are there things you do not understand?

  - ☐ If so, pray and read the verses again. Read the verses before and after and see if they become clear. There may be some notes in your Bible that will help you.

  - ☐ Look for key references to other parts of the Bible. These are important to help us to see the bigger picture of what God means.

- Are there any verses from other books of the Bible included?

  - ☐ This happens many times in the New Testament. If so, look the verses up in the Old Testament passage.

Why?
Why is it said?

- What does the writer want the hearer to think or believe or do?

- What difference did it make to God's people?

- What does it teach us about Jesus? (Remember, all the Bible is about Jesus!)

Example—Genesis 12:1-9

Who is in the passage?

☐ *The L*ORD *is talking to Abram (Abraham).*

☐ *Abraham is 75 years old and married to Sarai (Sarah). They have no children (11:30) but their brother's son Lot is with them.*

☐ *Verse 1 says: "The L*ORD *had said…". Verse 7 says: "The L*ORD *appeared to Abram and said…". These verses are about what God said to Abraham. They will explain why Abraham left his home in Ur to go to Canaan.*

What is it about?

☐ *God makes a promise to Abraham. Notice "bless" and "blessing" in v2, and "bless" and "blessed" in v3. The promise is to bless, which means to do good things for Abraham.*

  ☐ *God promises to:*
    ☐ *make Abraham into a great nation*
    ☐ *make Abraham's name great*
    ☐ *bless peoples all round the world through Abraham.*

☐ Remember what we saw in **BACKGROUND**. God's promises to Abraham and the peoples of the world show God's great love and kindness. Abraham is a sinner. He lives in a world of sinners. He lives in a world under God's judgment. But God is full of grace. God promises to do good things to people who deserve his judgment.

☐ In verse 7 we read that part of God's promise is to give Abraham's family the land of Canaan—which is why it is called the Promised Land.

☐ What does Abraham do?

  ☐ Abraham left his country because God told him to. He did not know where he was going. He trusted God's promise.

  ☐ Abraham worshipped God (v7-8) because God appeared to him and gave him a big promise. Abraham hears God, sees God and worships God.

Why is it said?

☐ Remember, this is in the Old Testament. The Israelites read this when they were in the desert. This passage reminded the Israelites that **God** had a plan to make them his people and bring them to the promised land. Like Abraham, they must trust God's promise and obey his word. They must worship God.

☐ **Read Hebrews 11:8-10.** This may be one of the references from Genesis 12:1-2 given at the bottom of the page in your Bible. (Hebrews 11 reminds us to live by faith: to trust God's promised plan and look forward to God's heavenly city.)

☐ **Read Galatians 3:16,** which tells us that the "offspring" or "child" God speaks about in Genesis 12:7 is Jesus. It is through Jesus that blessing will come to every nation. It is through Jesus that sinners can reach the promised land of heaven.

FIND THE MAIN POINT OF THE PASSAGE

Find the **MAIN POINT**. The **MAIN POINT** is the big thing God says in each passage. It is important that you find this **in** the passage. Some preachers decide what the big thing they want to say is before they start studying the verses! I heard a sermon where the preacher said a lot about giving money. The passage he preached from did not mention giving or money at all! He missed the **MAIN POINT**!

Look at the picture of the plane again.

There are many things that you could say about this picture. For example:

- The plane is small.
- The plane has three wheels and some windows.
- There are some people next to the plane.

However none of these things tell us the **big thing** that the picture shows. The big thing is that a sick person is being rescued and taken to receive more care.

Sometimes our sermons and talks are like that. They say many true things but they miss the **MAIN POINT**. Sometimes we want to say everything in a passage. We say so many things that nobody knows what the most important thing is!

The important question to ask is: What is the MAIN POINT, the big thing that these verses say?

Example—Genesis 12:1-9

☐ *In Genesis 12:1-9 we read that Abram called on the name of the LORD (v8) but that is not the **MAIN POINT** of the passage.*

☐ *The passage is about what the LORD said to Abram.*

To help you find the **MAIN POINT**, read through all you have written in **UNDERSTAND**. Think about the big thing that it says. Look for words or themes that are repeated. In the picture, the focus was on the sick person being taken onto the plane to get help.

What is the focus of the passage?

Write in one or two sentences what the passage is about.

Example—Genesis 12:1-9

☐ *God promises to bless Abraham even though he does not deserve it. God promises to give him a big family (great nation). God promises to take him to a new country and bless all peoples through him. Abraham responds with faith.*

Write out the **MAIN POINT** and then read the passage again. Make sure you did not leave out anything important.

PRACTICE

● *Now practise this for yourself. Go through the steps above and make some notes that will help you to build a sermon on Genesis 12:1-9.*

● *What do you think is the* **MAIN POINT**? *Write this in your own words.*

7. PLAN
HOW TO PLAN A SERMON FROM THE PASSAGE

In this chapter we learn:

- How to PLAN a talk on a passage of the Bible so our hearers will understand God's message.

- We must work hard to help our hearers follow and remember what we say.

If you make a meal for your family, you do not just put the vegetables on the table with a chicken. The vegetables are good. The meat is good. But you must prepare the vegetables. You must cook the meat. In the same way you have some ingredients for your sermon that will be food to your hearers. You have some notes on the passage. You have some good things to say—but this is not a sermon. It is not prepared and cooked yet!

Follow these steps to **plan** a sermon or talk:

MAIN POINT of the sermon → SUB-POINTS → ILLUSTRATE → APPLY → REVIEW

1. MAIN POINT OF THE SERMON

A sermon explains the passage, and it also applies the passage to the hearer. Look at the main point of the passage. Write out what this main point will mean for your hearer.

We must think what it meant for the people then—and then with God's help we must work out what it means for us today, many years later.

Example—Genesis 12:1-9

☐ **MAIN POINT of the passage:** *God promises to bless Abraham even though he does not deserve it. God promises to give him a big family (great nation). God promises to take him to a new country and bless all peoples through him. Abraham responds with faith.*

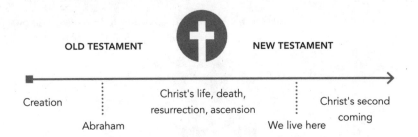

OLD TESTAMENT   NEW TESTAMENT

Creation   Christ's life, death, resurrection, ascension   Christ's second coming

Abraham   We live here

We cannot go straight from Abraham to us. We live after the death of Jesus on the cross, which makes a big difference.

The New Testament teaches that the promise to Abraham is fulfilled (comes true) in Jesus (Galatians 3:16). Through Jesus we can be part of God's big family, go to God's new country (heaven) and know the blessing of God with us. Like Abraham we must respond with faith. We saw this in Hebrews 11:8-10 in **UNDERSTAND** (on page 33).

A sermon will explain this and apply the message to their hearer. Write this, for example:

☐ **MAIN POINT of the sermon:** *God promises that through Jesus we can be part of God's family, go to God's new country, and know God's peace and blessing. We must respond with faith in Jesus.*

MAIN POINT of the sermon → SUB-POINTS → ILLUSTRATE → APPLY → REVIEW

Now you understand the passage. You have some notes and the **MAIN POINT**—but this is not a sermon or a talk! We need to **plan** the sermon or talk.

You put in one ingredient and then another and another.

Write the **MAIN POINT** of the sermon at the top of your paper. This will help you to **plan** a good message.

Many preachers do not **plan** their messages.

Some repeat the same point again and again, which becomes boring. They go round and round in circles! It is unhelpful—like being on a plane that goes round in circles but never lands!

Others have a lot to say but there is no plan. It is hard to follow—like being on a bus that goes to lots of places but never reaches where you want to go!

A good way to plan your message is to have two, three or four **SUB-POINTS** or headings. It makes it easy to follow. It is like following the recipe for your favourite soup. You put in one ingredient and then another and another. In the end you are satisfied with a good meal!

2. SUB-POINTS

SUB-POINTS explain a part of the **MAIN POINT**.

SUB-POINTS explain one part of the passage.

SUB-POINTS are short so your hearers can remember them.

Think how you will break the passage up.

- What verses go with each of the **SUB-POINTS**?

- Are all the verses covered?

- How can you make the **SUB-POINTS** follow on from each other to make the main point as clear as possible

- Are the **SUB-POINTS** short and easy to remember?

Example—Genesis 12:1-9

□ *The MAIN POINT of the sermon is:* God promises we can be part of God's family, go to God's new country and know God's peace and blessing. We must respond with faith in Jesus.

□ *From this, the* **SUB-POINTS** *might be:*

1. The promise of God's big family (v1-3)
2. The journey of faith to God's great country (v4-5)
3. The blessing of knowing God (v6-9)

Notice that all of the **SUB-POINTS**:

- explain a part of the **MAIN POINT**.

- have "God" in each one. The passage is all about God!

- explain a part of the passage.

In the example there are three **SUB-POINTS**, but you might have two or four **SUB-POINTS**. Each passage is different. Each sermon is different. Sometimes you will have two points, three points or four points—but they must always explain the **MAIN POINT**.

3. ILLUSTRATE OR TELL A STORY

An **ILLUSTRATION** or a word picture helps your hearers understand the **MAIN POINTS** you make. Sometimes there are **ILLUSTRATIONS** in the passage. For example, Paul uses the picture of an athlete, who has to train hard and keep the rules. (2 Timothy 2:5, 4:7)

Sometimes you need to think of your own **ILLUSTRATION**. Make sure the **ILLUSTRATION** is easy to understand and relates to the life of your people.

Example—Genesis 12:1-9

The message is that we must have faith in the promise of God. Your main **ILLUSTRATION** or story will explain faith to your hearers.

- ☐ *If you travel on a bus or a boat, you ask the driver where the bus or boat is going. On some buses there is a sign on the front to tell you. When you get on the bus, you have faith that the bus will take you to the right place. You trust the word of the driver.*

- ☐ *Abraham had faith in God. God promised he will take him to a new country. Abraham did not know the way or where he was going. He trusted God to lead him.*

You could take a visual aid or picture. You could draw a picture or do a short drama. Always make sure it helps to teach the **MAIN POINT**!

4. APPLY

When we teach God's word, we want God's word to speak to us and change all who hear it. So you must think how the **MAIN POINT** of the passage **APPLIES** to the people **you** are speaking to.

We must remember the timeline (see page 37), especially when we teach from the Old Testament. We live after Jesus, so we must look back to the Old Testament through the cross.

Think of the different people that you will speak to. How does the **MAIN POINT** speak to:

- children
- new believers
- those who are not believers
- church leaders

Think about the questions your listeners will have as they listen. For example:

- What will this mean for me tomorrow?
- How do I put this into practice in this church?
- How will I obey this in my family?
- How will I live this in my village or community?
- How does this help me to follow Jesus faithfully?
- What dangers do I need to be aware of?

You can **APPLY** the message after each **SUB-POINT** and at the end. If you only **APPLY** the message at the end, some may not hear it.

Example—Genesis 12:1-9

☐ *Abraham had faith in God. Many people think they will get to heaven because they are good or they go to church. This is wrong. The message of the Bible is that we are saved by faith. The message of the Bible is that God promises heaven to those who have faith in Jesus.*

☐ *Abraham did not know where he was going. There are many things we do not know about the future. We must trust God's word and his promises.*

☐ *God promised to bless Abraham. Many Christians think this means God will give them money and possessions. God did **not** promise Abraham money. The promise is about God's family and God's heaven. We must help our hearers to remember that the blessings we have in Jesus are spiritual blessings. The blessing of being in God's family. The blessing of going to heaven. These blessings are more precious than money.*

You now have notes about the passage and a PLAN for how you will share God's message. These will help you to make your sermon.

5. REVIEW

Before you teach, you must **REVIEW** your PLAN.

- Check what you prepared:

  o Is the **MAIN POINT** clear?

  o Do you show what the Bible teaches in **that** passage?

  o Have you explained the verses clearly?

  o Have you thought of word pictures to help people understand and remember the message?

  o Do you have a clear flow to your talk so that people can follow what you say?

  o What are you asking God to change in the lives of your hearers?

- Decide if you will speak using a sermon you wrote out fully or use shorter notes.

- Always use the language most of your hearers will understand best. Think carefully about language. Which language will you speak in? What will your hearers best understand? What notes will best help you to speak in that language?

PRACTICE

- *Now practise this for yourself. Go through the steps above and make some notes that will help you to PLAN a sermon on Genesis 12:1-9.*

- *Write out your own PLAN, including **SUB-POINTS** in your own words and language.*

8. TEACH
HOW TO WRITE A SERMON OR TALK FROM THE PASSAGE

In this chapter we learn:

- How to prepare notes to TEACH a passage of the Bible clearly.
- It is important to prepare EVERY part of our sermon or talk.

These steps will help you write a sermon or talk.

START → EXPLAIN → ILLUSTRATE → APPLY → END → PRAY

This section will help you write a sermon or talk on the Bible passage. It is **not** a complete sermon. You will need to do your own work as well—but it gives you ideas. You must take the ideas and use them in the best way for you.

Always remember that the talk is based on the **MAIN POINT**.

1. START
When will you read the passage? Will you ask someone else to read it?

Think carefully about how to **START** your talk. You need to get the people's interest so that they listen. It is good to tell your people the **MAIN POINT**. Tell them why they need to listen and how this passage will help them. You can ask a question and tell them you will answer it in your talk. Sometimes you may begin with a small drama or visual aid or story.

Example—Genesis 12:1-9

☐ *The MAIN POINT of the sermon is:* God promises we can be part of God's family, go to God's new country, and know God's peace and blessing. We must respond with faith in Jesus.

☐ *Ask your hearers: What is faith? What does it mean to have faith or to walk by faith? Read Hebrews 11:8. Say to your hearers that we will look at Abraham to help us understand what it means to have faith.*

---

2. EXPLAIN

SUB-POINTS are like bones in a body. Bones keep you standing up straight. But you also need flesh or meat! You need to take time to **EXPLAIN** the verses, to put meat on the bones. You need to make clear what the verses mean. It is good to keep reading the verses from the Bible as you **EXPLAIN** them. Get your people to follow in their Bibles.

This book gives you some ideas, but you will also need to add your own. Think what is good for your people and what will help them to understand clearly.

Make sure your hearers can see that what you say **is** what the Bible says!

Example—Genesis 12:1-9

1. The promise of God's big family (v1-3)

God tells Abram (or Abraham) to do something very hard. Read verse 1. His family have lived in Ur for a very long time. All his relatives are in Ur. All his friends are in Ur. Everything he knows is in Ur. Why does he leave? Because God promises him something better. Read verses 2-3. Three times God says: "I will…" God is making a promise to Abraham. God says: "I will bless you". This is not about money—Abraham already has a lot of possessions. God promises him something he **does not** have. He promises Abraham the blessing of being the first member of a new nation or family. God promises that everyone in this nation will be blessed, and that this family will be people from all the different nations of the world. It will be a great family—God's family. God tells Abraham to leave his own country and family because God promises him a better country and a better family. The Old Testament tells the story of this family—the people of Israel (Israel is another name for Abraham's grandson, Jacob). But this was only a small part of what God promised Abraham. Read Galatians 3:16, which tells us the "offspring" or "child" God speaks about in Genesis 12:7 is Jesus. It is through Jesus we can be part of God's big family. It is a family of people from every nation. It is the best family—a blessed family, God's family.

2. The journey of faith to God's great country (v4-5)

Tell what happens in verses 4-5. Abraham is not a young man. He takes **everything** he has. Abraham does not plan to go back to Ur. He trusts God's promise and **fully** obeys what God told him to do. It is not enough to know what God promises. We must have faith. We must respond to what God says. Abraham had to leave his own country to arrive in the promised land of Canaan. He did not know how to get there. He did not know how hard it would be. He trusted God. Read Hebrews 11:8-10. Hebrews 11 reminds us to live by faith: to trust God's promised plan and look forward to God's heavenly city.

Use your main **ILLUSTRATION**.

3. The blessing of knowing God (v6-9)

Abraham has faith in God. He leaves his own country and goes to the land God promised. When he arrives, it is already full of people—the Canaanites! (Read verse 6.) They will not give their land to Abraham. Abraham does not have an army. How can this land ever be his home? God appears to Abraham. Abraham met God and heard God. We do not know what Abraham saw but we do know what he heard. God repeats the promise again (read verse 7). God says: "Yes, I will keep my promise". Abraham builds an altar—he worships God. He does the same at Bethel (Bethel means "house of God"). Abraham is living with God! God promises that Abraham will be God's friend. This is the biggest blessing in the world: to know God, to hear God, to talk to God, to pray to God, to be cared for by God, to love God. Through Jesus YOU can enjoy this blessing! If you trust in Jesus, one day you will be with God in heaven!

3. ILLUSTRATE

In the PLAN section we thought of one main illustration. You may need to think of others also. Sometimes a word picture is better than a long story. When we get on a bus or boat, we trust the driver to take us to the place he says. Abraham trusted God to lead him—even though he did not know where he would go.

Example—Genesis 12:1-9

   ☐ *The Christian life is like a journey—the journey of faith. We can trust God to take us on this journey and bring us in the end to be with him in heaven.*

4. APPLY

In the PLAN section we thought how to **APPLY** the passage. It is important to make this as clear as possible. Give your hearers something to think about, or something to do. Remember we want people to change and grow. Make sure you remember to say something to those who are not believers. You always have different groups of people listening:

- Believers who are full of faith

- Believers who feel like giving up

- Unbelievers who want to become Christians but do not know how

- Unbelievers who do not think they need to be saved.

Try and say something to each one! Everyone needs to hear something.

Example—Genesis 12:1-9

To believers who are full of faith:

☐ *Look forward to heaven. God has promised he will take you home. You cannot see heaven. You do not know how good it will be but you can trust God's promise. You can enjoy a taste of heaven now as you hear God in the Bible and worship God with his people.*

To believers who feel like giving up:

☐ *Abraham had many problems. God promised him a big family but his wife could not have children. Abraham had to trust God when it seemed impossible. Will you trust God to help you?*

To unbelievers who want to become Christians but do not know how:

☐ *Abraham did not know where he was going—but when God called him he obeyed. He trusted God, and God was faithful to him. Will you trust God? You will find he will be faithful to you. Believe in Jesus today!*

To unbelievers who do not think they need to be saved:

☐ *Abraham worshipped other gods. He did not know God, but God called to him and promised him something better. God calls you to repent and believe in Jesus because it is better!*

☐ *Abraham left his home and his family. It was hard but it was worth it! If you do not have faith in God, you will be punished. The Bible says that only those who have faith go to heaven. Everyone else goes to hell.*

5. END

Think how to **END** your talk. Remind your hearers of the **MAIN POINT**. Help them to remember.

Sometimes it is helpful after speaking to give your hearers time to think and pray about what they heard before you carry on with the meeting.

Example—Genesis 12:1-9

☐ *God called Abraham to leave his country and go to the promised land. Abraham trusted and obeyed God. Today God calls you. God is willing to make you part of his family. God is able to bring you to his heavenly promised land. God can give you a wonderful relationship with him. Will you turn to God now and put all your trust in him?*

6. PRAY

PRAY and keep praying.

- **PRAY** God will first change you.

- **PRAY** God will use your words to speak to your people.

- **PRAY** God's truth will change your people.

Example—Genesis 12:1-9

☐ *PRAY God will help your hearers understand the blessing of knowing God through Jesus.*

☐ *PRAY God will help you and your hearers to have faith in Jesus, and to obey everything he calls you to do.*

PRACTICE

- *Now practise this for yourself. Go through the steps above and make some notes that will help you to preach a sermon on Genesis 12:1-9.*

- *Think about **who** will be your hearers. How will you **APPLY** it to them? Write this out in your own words and language.*

- *Do not forget to **REVIEW** your notes before you preach. Is the **MAIN POINT** clear?*

9. PRACTICE OUTLINE

We hope you see how this method helps you to dig deeper into the Bible and to explain God's message clearly for your people.

This may be something new for you and may seem very hard. The important thing is to practise. Then it will get clearer and easier.

- Follow the **same** steps—Study—Plan—Teach for a talk or sermon on **Mark 6:30-44**.

- Some answers can be found in "Extra" at the end of the book. Write your **own** answers **before** you read the answers.

Here are the steps to follow. For more help read chapters 5 – 8 again.

STUDY—how to understand the passage

BACKGROUND

To understand the **BACKGROUND** you need to think about:

The whole Bible

- Where in the story of the Bible does this book come? (Look at the timeline on page 37.)

- Is it in the Old Testament (before Jesus came) or in the New Testament (when or after Jesus came)?

- When in history is this book set? (The Bible story is the true history of the world.)

The whole book
- Who wrote the book?
- Who was the book written for?

The passage before the one you will speak from
- Where is it in the book?
- What is the main point of the passage before this one?

READ
Read the Bible passage **three times**. Read it slowly and carefully. It is best to read out loud. Read it in a different translation if you have one. The third time, read it with your eyes and ears, your nose and hands! Imagine you were there. What will you see, hear, smell and feel?

What words are difficult? Try and work out what they mean. Is there someone you can ask to help you? Can you look in a dictionary?

UNDERSTAND
Here are some questions to ask:

Who?
Who is in this passage?
- What do you learn about each of the people?
- What do you learn about where they are?
- What does this passage say about God (Father, Jesus and Holy Spirit)?

What?
What is it about?
- Are any words or ideas repeated?
- Are there things you do not understand?
  - ☐ If so, pray and read the verses again. Read the verses before and after and see if they become clear.
  - ☐ Look for key references to other parts of the Bible. These are important to help us to see the bigger picture of what God means.
- Are there any verses from other books of the Bible included?
  - ☐ This happens many times in the New Testament. If so, look the verses up in the Old Testament passage.

Why?
Why is it said?

- What does the writer want the hearer to think or believe or do?

- What difference did it make to God's people?

- What does it teach us about Jesus? (Remember, all the Bible is about Jesus!)

FIND THE MAIN POINT OF THE PASSAGE

The **MAIN POINT** is the big thing God says in each passage. It is important that you find this in the passage. To help you find the main point, read through all you have written in UNDERSTAND. Think about the big thing that it says. Look for words or themes that are repeated.

Write in one or two sentences what the passage is about.

PLAN—how to plan a sermon from the passage

MAIN POINT OF THE SERMON

A sermon explains the passage, and it also applies the passage to the hearer. Look at the **MAIN POINT** of the passage. Write what this **MAIN POINT** will mean for *your* hearers.

SUB-POINTS

SUB-POINTS explain a part of the **MAIN POINT**.

SUB-POINTS explain one part of the passage.

SUB-POINTS are short so your hearers can remember them.

Think how you will break the passage up.

- What verses go with each of the **SUB-POINTS**?

- Are all the verses covered?

- How can you make the **SUB-POINTS** follow on from each other to make the main point as clear as possible?

- Are the **SUB-POINTS** short and easy to remember?

ILLUSTRATE OR TELL A STORY

An **ILLUSTRATION** or a word picture helps your hearers understand the **MAIN POINTS** you make. You could take a visual aid or picture. You could draw a picture or do a short drama. Always make sure it helps to teach the **MAIN POINT**!

APPLY

Think of the different people that you will speak to. Think about the questions your listeners will have as they listen. For example:

- What will this mean for me tomorrow?
- How do I put this into practice in this church?
- How will I obey this in my family?
- How will I live this in my village or community?
- How does this help me to follow Jesus faithfully?
- What dangers do I need to be aware of?

REVIEW

Before you teach you must **REVIEW** your plan.

- Check what you prepared:
  - Is the main point clear?
  - Do you show what the Bible teaches in THAT passage?
  - Have you explained the verses clearly?
  - Have you thought of word pictures to help people understand and remember the message?
  - Do you have a clear flow to your talk so that people can follow what you say?
  - What are you asking God to change in the lives of your hearers?
- Decide if you will speak using a sermon you wrote out fully or use shorter notes.
- Always use the language most of your hearers will understand best. Think carefully about language. Which language will you speak in? What will your hearers best understand? What notes will best help you to speak in that language?

TEACH—how to write a sermon or talk from the passage

START

When will you read the passage? Will you ask someone else to read it?

Think carefully about how to **START** your talk. You need to get the people's interest so that they listen. It is good to tell your people the **MAIN POINT**. Tell them why they need to listen and how this passage will help them.

EXPLAIN

You need to make clear what the verses mean. It is good to keep reading the verses from the Bible as you **EXPLAIN** them. Make sure your hearers can see that what you say **is** what the Bible says!

ILLUSTRATE

In the PLAN section we thought of one main **ILLUSTRATION**. You may need to think of others also.

APPLY

Make sure you remember to say something to those who are not believers. You always have different groups of people listening:

- Believers who are full of faith
- Believers who feel like giving up
- Unbelievers who want to become Christians but do not know how
- Unbelievers who do not think they need to be saved

Try and say something to each one! Everyone needs to hear something.

END

Think how to **END** your talk. Remind your hearers of the **MAIN POINT**. Help them to remember.

Sometimes it is helpful after speaking to give your hearers time to think and pray about what they heard before you carry on with the meeting.

PRAY

PRAY and keep praying.

- **PRAY** God will first change you
- **PRAY** God will use your words to speak to your people.
- **PRAY** God's truth will change your people.

Keep on using this outline to prepare your sermons.

10. PREACH

This book is in a series called "Pray Prepare **Preach**".

- We have seen how to PREPARE a sermon. Now it is important to think how to PREACH the sermon.

- In this chapter we will think about how to PREACH the message so people understand what we say and are changed by God's word.

Read 2 Corinthians 4:1-6:

> [1]Therefore, since through God's mercy we have this ministry, we do not lose heart. [2]Rather, we have renounced secret and shameful ways; we do not use deception, nor do we distort the word of God. On the contrary, by setting forth the truth plainly we commend ourselves to everyone's conscience in the sight of God. [3]And even if our gospel is veiled, it is veiled to those who are perishing. [4]The god of this age has blinded the minds of unbelievers, so that they cannot see the light of the gospel that displays the glory of Christ, who is the image of God. [5]For what we preach is not ourselves, but Jesus Christ as Lord, and ourselves as your servants for Jesus' sake. [6]For God, who said, "Let light shine out of darkness," made his light shine in our hearts to give us the light of the knowledge of God's glory displayed in the face of Christ.

- *What does Paul say he does **not** do? (v2, 5)*

- *What does Paul say he **does** do? (v2, 5)*

There is a big difference between a bad sermon and a good sermon. Read through the verses again and see if you find a verse which shows these differences:

A BAD SERMON...	A GOOD SERMON...
"distorts" or twists the word of God.	clearly teaches what the Bible says.
is all about the preacher.	is all about Jesus.
puts pressure on people to do what the preacher says.	is used by the Holy Spirit to do God's work.

PREACHING:

1. tells out God's word **clearly** so people can understand God's greatness.

2. shows what the Bible says about **Jesus** so people can see how precious Jesus is.

3. applies the Bible so that the Holy Spirit **changes** people to the praise of God.

Let us think about these three statements.

Speak clearly

Preaching tells out God's word clearly so people can understand God's greatness.

If we want people to understand the Bible, we must speak clearly. Some preachers speak so quickly that people cannot understand what they say. Some preachers are so quiet that people at the back cannot hear! We must speak clearly. We must speak carefully. We must show that what we say is what the Bible says. This means we must read the verses many times as we explain them so that our hearers can clearly see that what we say **is** what the Bible says.

Most preachers find it helpful to use their sermon notes when they preach. It has taken many hours to understand the passage and prepare the sermon, and our notes will help us to explain clearly what the passage says. You will want your notes in the same language you will speak.

Speak about Jesus

Show what the Bible says about Jesus so people can see how precious Jesus is.

Paul says that the truth about Jesus is "treasure" (2 Corinthians 4:7). The good news about Jesus is the most exciting, important news. If we love Jesus and the truth about Jesus, it must show when we speak about him.

Preaching must show our love for God and also our love for people. Think about the people you preach to. Some will be very sad; some will have doubts and fears. We must speak the truth with love. We must be kind in the way that we speak. Some people need to be corrected. We must speak clearly and boldly but show love for them and not anger.

It is important to **look** at the people as you preach. It is good to use sermon notes when we preach but we must not read them without looking at our hearers. Looking at our hearers will help them to listen to us, and to see our love for God and them.

Speak for change
Apply the Bible so the Holy Spirit changes people to the praise of God.

A sermon explains and applies the Bible. A sermon helps people understand the Bible and understand *what they must do*. We must help people to believe the message, to obey the message. We must help our hearers to understand why they should believe and change. We can plead with them and warn them. In 2 Corinthians 5:20 Paul says: *"We implore you on Christ's behalf: be reconciled to God"*. But we cannot change people's hearts. We cannot make people believe. Only God's Spirit can do this. As we preach, we must pray for God to work through our words.

Only God can change people's hearts, but the exciting thing is that God uses sermons and Bible studies to do his great work! God uses us!

THINK
What was the last sermon or talk that you gave? Think about each of these questions and **write** down your answers.

- *What notes did you use?*
- *Did you talk about Jesus? What did you say?*
- *Did you look at the people you were speaking to?*
- *Did you pray for yourself and your hearers to be changed by the message?*
- *What will you do **differently** next time?*

FIND OUT

Before you speak next time, ask a friend in your church to take notes on your sermon or talk.

A few days afterwards, sit down with the person and ask them to go through their notes with you. Pray together and then discuss these questions:

● *What was the **MAIN POINT**?*

● *Did you explain the passage clearly?*

● *Did you speak too quickly, quietly or loudly?*

● *What illustrations did you use? Did they help explain the **MAIN POINT**?*

● *What did God tell them through his word to think, say or do?*

11. THE MAIN POINT: TEACH THE BIBLE

What is the message, the main point, of this book? It is **TEACH THE BIBLE!**

- Teach the Bible with care.

- Teach the Bible to yourself.

- Teach the Bible to everybody.

- Teach the Bible with prayer.

Paul says: *"We have this treasure in jars of clay to show that this all-surpassing power is from God and not from us"* (2 Corinthians 4:7).

The treasure Paul talks about is the message about Jesus—the treasure of the gospel, the life-changing message of Christ and his cross. Preaching and teaching God's word is a big responsibility—we are passing on God's treasure! But we are so weak and sinful. We have many battles and struggles. We suffer and are broken. We are like jars of clay—cheap pots that you buy in the market, or like plastic bags that you use once and then throw away.

We cannot make anyone become a Christian. We cannot change people's lives—we are too weak. But the power is not from us but from God.

It is good to know we are weak because we will rely on God and not on ourselves.

It is good to know we are weak because, when God uses us to help people, we will praise God and not become proud.

Preaching and teaching the Bible is hard work. It takes time to pray and prepare. It is hard to live out God's word so people see in us the things we say. It takes sacrifice and pain, but preaching and teaching the Bible is the best work in the world!

I can think of times when God spoke to me as I prepared to preach. God showed me my sin, and I stopped studying and got down on my knees and prayed. At other times, as I read the Bible, I started to sing as I learned something wonderful about Jesus.

There is nothing more wonderful than seeing people become Christians because we preach the Bible to them and God uses it in their lives. There are people who are in heaven now because they heard the Bible through us. That is amazing. That is God at work!

Study the Bible. Listen to the Bible. Preach the Bible. Teach the Bible. God will use his word in your life and the lives of other people to do great things!

I pray God will make you the preacher **he** wants you to be so that you will be used to bring great honour to his name. Will you pray this too?

Here are some questions to help you think about the lessons in this book:

- *Will you make sure preaching the Bible is the most important part of your church meetings each Sunday?*

- *Will you preach from **all** the Bible, showing it is all about Jesus?*

- *Will you pray for the Holy Spirit to use the Bible to change people's lives?*

- *Will you give more time to prepare to teach and preach, using the pattern in this book?*

- *What part of your life needs to change so that you live the message of the Bible?*

- *Will you ask God to make you the preacher **he** wants you to be?*

PRACTICE EXAMPLE— MARK 6:30-44

Here are some answers to the Practice on page 47.

Make sure that you have written your **own** answers **before** you read the answers that are given.

STUDY—how to understand the passage

BACKGROUND
What is the BACKGROUND to the passage from the whole Bible?

- ☐ Mark is one of the four Gospels.

- ☐ Mark tells about the life, death and resurrection of Jesus.

What is the BACKGROUND to the passage from the whole book?

- ☐ Mark is probably "John Mark", who we read about in Acts (for example 12:12).

- ☐ Mark tells us why he wrote his book in Mark 1:1 ("The beginning of the good news about Jesus the Messiah, the Son of God"). Mark is not only the life story of Jesus, but the message of who Jesus is and why Jesus came.

- ☐ The miracle of Jesus feeding the 5000 is told in all four Gospels. This shows how important it is (Matthew 14:13-21, Luke 9:10-17, John 6:1-15).

What is the BACKGROUND to the passage from the passage before and after Mark 6:30-44?

- ☐ Mark 6:1-6 tells how people in Jesus' home town reject the preaching of Jesus. They do not realise who Jesus is.

☐ Mark 6:14-29 tells how King Herod rejects the preaching of John the Baptist, who prepared the way for Jesus, and kills him.

☐ Mark 6:7, 30. The disciples have come back from a mission trip, and many people in the towns and villages have heard about Jesus, but do they realise who Jesus is?

☐ Mark 6:45-46 says Jesus and his disciples leave quickly. The people have seen a miracle but do not realise who Jesus is and why he has come. (Read also John 6:14-15.)

☐ Mark 6:47-52 says the disciples do not realise that Jesus is God.

READ
What words are difficult?

☐ "Solitary place" (v32) means a quiet place outside the town. The same Greek word is translated "quiet place" (v31) and "remote place" (v35).

☐ "Sheep without a shepherd" (v34). A shepherd is a farmer who looks after sheep. Sheep need a shepherd to lead them and care for them.

☐ The "five loaves" (v38) were very small pieces of bread. John tells us the five loaves and two fish were the dinner for one boy (John 6:9).

UNDERSTAND
Who is in the passage?

☐ The apostles (disciples):

  ☐ they have come back from preaching in the towns and villages. They are very tired and need a rest.

  ☐ they think it is impossible to feed so many people.

☐ The crowd:

  ☐ 5000 men have heard about Jesus and come to him.

  ☐ Jesus sees they need a shepherd or leader. In Numbers 27:15-17 Moses prays that God's people will not be like "a sheep without a shepherd". Jesus is the leader the people need.

☐ The passage is all about Jesus.

  ☐ Jesus is concerned about his disciples (v31).

  ☐ Jesus has compassion on the 5000 men who come (v34).

  ☐ Jesus does not send the people away but feeds them.

What is the passage about?

- □ Jesus teaches the people.

- □ Jesus feeds 5000 men (plus women and children—Matthew 14:21) with a small amount of food.

- □ After everyone has enough to eat there are twelve baskets filled with food.

- □ The miracle of feeding a big crowd in a lonely place reminds us of the way God fed his people in the wilderness with manna in the time of Moses (Exodus 16). God showed he was strong and could bring his people through hard places to the promised land.

Why is it said and what does it say about Jesus?

- □ This miracle is about who Jesus is.

- □ Jesus wants the people to see that he is the Shepherd leader they need. Jesus wants the disciples to understand he is the Son of God.

- □ Jesus does not promise to give us miracle food. Jesus does not promise to give us money, possessions and good health. The miracle teaches us to trust in Jesus because he is God.

- □ The miracle does not teach us that we must give food to people who are starving. It teaches us that Jesus can give us something more important. God fed the people with manna in the wilderness in Exodus to show he was with them and will bring them to the promised land. Jesus feeds 5000 men in a desert with a small amount of food to show we can trust him to bring us to the promised land of heaven.

FIND THE MAIN POINT OF THE PASSAGE
What is the MAIN POINT, the big thing these verses say?

- □ Jesus shows compassion for the people—he teaches them and then he feeds them. The miracle shows Jesus is God and the disciples must trust him.

PLAN—how to plan a sermon from the passage

MAIN POINT OF THE SERMON
Look at the main point of the passage. Write what this main point will mean for your hearers.

- □ Jesus is the caring leader of God's people. Trust Jesus, the Son of God, to satisfy you.

SUB-POINTS
How will you break the passage up?

1. *Jesus is the caring leader (v30-34)*

2. *Jesus can satisfy (v35-44)*

ILLUSTRATE OR TELL A STORY
Think of an illustration or a word picture that helps your hearers understand the main point.

☐ *The message is to see how great Jesus is. To understand this miracle it is helpful to tell the story of how God fed his people in Exodus with manna (Exodus 16). God showed that he cared for his people and was able to provide for them and bring them to the promised land.*

APPLY
How does the MAIN POINT of the passage apply to the people YOU are speaking to?

☐ *The people come to Jesus—they do not know what they need. They need Jesus to show them that he is the good shepherd. Help your hearers to see that they need Jesus. Are they listening to Jesus?*

☐ *Jesus feeds them as God fed his people in the desert with manna. Jesus is God. Help your hearers to see how great Jesus is and to turn to him.*

☐ *Jesus feeds them and they are satisfied. There are twelve baskets left over. Help your hearers to know that Jesus is able to help them and give them strength to keep serving him until they reach the promised land of heaven. They can trust him.*

TEACH—how to write a sermon or talk from the passage

START
How will you start your talk?

☐ *The **MAIN POINT** of the sermon: Jesus is the caring leader of God's people. Trust Jesus to satisfy you.*

☐ *To start, ask your hearers what will satisfy them? Talk about the things that people think will satisfy them: money, sex, food, pleasure. Tell your hearers that this passage tells them that only Jesus can truly satisfy.*

EXPLAIN
Write your sub-points and think how you will explain the passage to your hearers.

1. Jesus is the caring leader (v30-34)

☐ *The disciples are very tired—Jesus takes them to have a rest.*

☐ *The crowds come to Jesus—Jesus has compassion on them.*

☐ *"Sheep without a shepherd"—the people are lost. They have no one to teach them the truth and show them the right way.*

☐ *Numbers 27:15-17—Jesus is the promised leader the people need.*

☐ *Jesus cares for them by teaching them. Jesus cares for us by teaching us! We must listen to his words carefully.*

2. Jesus can satisfy (v35-44)

☐ *It is late and Jesus and his disciples are very tired but Jesus does not send the crowds home—he feeds them.*

☐ *Tell the story of the miracle, explaining how amazing it is.*

☐ *The miracle shows who Jesus is—he is God.*

☐ *The miracle took place in a remote or desert place. This reminds us of the manna in the wilderness—use your main illustration.*

☐ *Jesus wants the people to see that he is the Shepherd Leader they need. Jesus wants the disciples to understand he is the Son of God.*

☐ *Jesus does not promise to give us miracle food. Jesus does not promise to give us money, possessions and good health. The miracle teaches us to trust in Jesus because he is God.*

ILLUSTRATE
In the PLAN section we thought of one main illustration. You may need to think of others also.

☐ *The miracle is to show the people who Jesus is. It is a sign to teach them— it is like a road sign. It shows the way to go. It shows us to trust in Jesus.*

APPLY
You always have different groups of people listening. What will you say to each one?

To believers who are full of faith:

☐ *Make time to listen to Jesus. He can teach you more about himself.*

☐ *Bring others to Jesus to receive life from him.*

To believers who feel like giving up:

☐ *Look how great Jesus is. You cannot keep going in your strength but Jesus is strong enough. He is the bread of life—food for your soul! Trust him.*

To unbelievers who want to become Christians but do not know how:

☐ *Do not come to Jesus for miracles of healing and money. Jesus came for your biggest need—he came as the good shepherd to lay down his life for you so your sins can be forgiven (John 10:11).*

To unbelievers who do not think they need to be saved:

☐ *Money, food and sex cannot satisfy us. We always want more. But Jesus can satisfy our biggest need—our need for forgiveness for sin. He is God. If you reject him you will be rejected by him on the Day of Judgment.*

END
Think how to end your talk.

☐ *Money, sex, food and pleasure can never satisfy us. They are like bread— soon we will be hungry again. But Jesus came to meet our real needs. We need him. He is the bread of life. Jesus satisfies for ever.*

PRAY
☐ *Ask God to show your hearers that only Jesus can truly satisfy.*

☐ *Ask God to help them be more excited by Jesus than by miracles.*

REVIEW
Before you teach it, you must review what you wrote.

thegoodbook
COMPANY
Opening up the Bible

At The Good Book Company, we are dedicated to helping people understand what Christianity is, and to helping Christians and local churches grow. We believe that God's growth process always starts with hearing clearly what he has said to us through his timeless word—the Bible.

Ever since we opened our doors in 1991, we have been striving to produce resources that honour God in the way the Bible is used. We have grown to become an international provider of user-friendly resources, with people of all backgrounds and denominations using our books, courses and DVDs.

We want to enable people to understand who Jesus is; and to equip ordinary Christians to live for him day by day, and churches to grow in their knowledge of God and in their love for one another and their neighbours.

Call us for a discussion of your needs or visit one of our local websites for more information on the resources and services we provide.

UK & Europe: www.thegoodbook.co.uk
North America: www.thegoodbook.com
Australia: www.thegoodbook.com.au
New Zealand: www.thegoodbook.co.nz

UK & Europe: 0333 123 0880
North America: 866 244 2165
Australia: (02) 6100 4211
New Zealand (+64) 3 343 1990

www.christianityexplored.org

Our partner site is a great place for those exploring the Christian faith, with a clear explanation of the good news, powerful testimonies and answers to difficult questions.

One life. What's it all about?